MW01600314

Let's Go to Church!

A GUIDE TO GETTING THE MOST OUT OF LORD'S DAY SERVICES AND ENCOURAGING YOUR SPIRITUAL LEADERS

Nancy DeMoss Wolgemuth

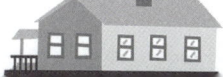

©2022 *Revive Our Hearts*

Published by *Revive Our Hearts*
P.O. Box 2000, Niles, MI 49120

ISBN 978-1-934718-93-3

Printed in the United States of America

Edited by Erin Davis, Katie Laitkep, Mindi Stearns, and Mindy Kroesche.

Design by Austin Collins.

CONTENTS

INTRODUCTION

When we find ourselves bored or distracted during the preaching of the Word or we feel like the messages aren't impacting our lives, our tendency is to blame the preacher. However, the problem may not be so much with the one teaching the Word as with the one listening. As you learn from your pastor, Bible study leaders, and Sunday school teachers, ask yourself: **Do I have a readiness to hear, receive, and respond to the Word?**

The fact is, two people can listen to the same message and one be bored and unmoved and the other convicted and his or her life transformed. What makes the difference? **The condition of our hearts.** The most anointed preaching will make little impact on a hardened or preoccupied heart. But a receptive, prepared, responsive heart can find life and grace every time the Word of God is proclaimed.

The Church is more than a building. It goes beyond just a place we go. The Church is the people of God who gather

6

each Lord's Day for worship and edification, then scatter to be living letters (2 Cor. 3:3), called to share the love of Christ with the world the rest of the week.

This guide is intended to help you grow in your love for God's Church and come alongside those who are leading in your church by becoming an active "hearer" and "doer"— ready to grow and to become more like Jesus.

But be doers of the word and not hearers only, deceiving yourselves. Because if anyone is a hearer of the word and not a doer, he is like someone looking at his own face in a mirror. For he looks at himself, goes away, and immediately forgets what kind of person he was. But the one who looks intently into the perfect law of freedom and perseveres in it, and is not a forgetful hearer but a doer who works—this person will be blessed in what he does. —James 1:22–25

7

HOW TO GET THE MOST OUT OF YOUR PASTOR'S PREACHING

Do you ever find yourself:

- Waking up on Sunday morning and wishing you didn't have to go to church?
- Having a hard time staying awake in church?
- Daydreaming during the message, or making a mental "to-do" list while the pastor is preaching?
- Picking apart the message or the preacher in your mind or not getting anything out of the sermon?
- Wishing your pastor would be more [fill in the blank]?
- Forgetting what the message was about before you get home from church?

If you're not benefitting from the ministry of the Word as it is publicly proclaimed in your local church, the fault may not lie in the one preaching but in your readiness to hear, receive, and respond. Here are some practical helps for preparing your heart to get the most out of your pastor's preaching.

Five Habits Before the Service

1. *Pray for your pastor* as he prepares for Sunday. Pray that:
   - His schedule would be free from unnecessary distractions.
   - God will give him understanding into the meaning of the Word.
   - The Holy Spirit will speak to him personally through the Word and that he will respond in humility and obedience.
   - God will help him to communicate the truth with clarity, freedom, passion, and power.

2. If your pastor is preaching a series from a particular book of the Bible, take time during the week to *read ahead and meditate on the text.* Ask God to speak to your heart before you even hear the message.

3. *Prepare for public worship the night before.* Consider shutting down your laptop, turning off the TV, and taking a break from social media; take time to cultivate your appetite for God's Word.

4. *Ask God to prepare your heart* for the preaching of the Word. Repent of any sin God reveals to you, and get

rid of the things that are standing in the way of the Word of God in your life.

5. *Come to church asking God to meet with you.* Expect to hear from Him and to be different when you leave.

Five Habits During the Service

1. *Be there.* You're not going to get anything out of church if you're not there. Don't be a sporadic attender; purpose to gather faithfully with God's people, if you are able.

2. *Get to church early.* Spend a few minutes before the service quietly preparing your heart for worship. Pray for God to move—in the pastor, in your heart, in others' hearts—and surrender your heart to whatever God will say.

3. *Don't be a spectator.* Participate fully in every part of the service. That means when it's time to sing—sing. When it's time to pray—pray. When it's time to give—give.

4. *Listen attentively and humbly* to the reading and the preaching of the Word. While the sermon is being preached, open your Bible or Bible app and follow along. If your pastor refers to other references, look them up. Try to make eye contact with the pastor. Be a "yes face." Not only does that help the pastor know people are listening and connecting, but it helps you stay alert and focused. Ask the Lord to make His

Word clear. If your heart is humble, your focus won't be on evaluating the message or how it's delivered; you will let the message evaluate you.

5. *Take notes.* Jot down things the Lord speaks to you about; highlight points the Spirit applies to your heart and life. Take those notes home, and work through them later.

Five Habits After the Service

1. *Pray for God* to keep the soil of your heart fertile so that after you've heard the Word your life would bear fruit (Mark 4:20).

2. *Ask God* to give you at least one takeaway from the message—a key concept, phrase, or verse that you can review throughout the week. Jot it down so you don't forget.

3. While it's still fresh on your mind (before you leave church, on the way home from church, over the meal following the service, etc.), *discuss the message with others.* Share how God spoke to you.

4. *Be a doer of the Word* and not just a hearer (James 1:22). Apply what you heard Sunday morning to real-life, everyday circumstances and situations throughout the week.

11

5. *Pray for your pastor.* He has poured out his time and energy so that the people in your congregation could be filled with God's Word. Pray that He would experience refreshment and be filled by the Spirit in the week ahead.

And One Don't . . .

Don't make your pastor a prisoner of unrealistic expectations. He doesn't have to be mesmerizing, entertaining, dramatic, or tell a lot of stories to be effective. You are blessed if he is a man of God who is humble, loves the Word, and opens the Word and seeks to make its meaning plain. The ultimate power is in the truth of Scripture, not in the messenger.

Five Prompts to Make It Personal

As you seek to better engage with the teaching of the Word in your church, consider the following questions and reflect on the Scripture references provided.

1. Do I highly esteem, respect, and revere the Word of God?

    • Nehemiah 8:5–6
    • Psalm 138:2

2. Do I prepare my heart to hear the Word of God?

   • Psalm 119:18
   • Job 11:13–19

3. Do I have a teachable spirit?

   • Psalm 25:9
   • Proverbs 12:1

4. When the Word is preached, am I conscious that I am not listening to the words of men but to the Word of God?

   • 1 Thessalonians 2:13
   • 2 Timothy 3:16

_____

_____

_____

5. Do I have a commitment to obey anything God shows me from His Word?

   • Matthew 7:24
   • James 1:22–25

_____

_____

_____

FOR THOSE WHO LISTEN TO THE TEACHING & PREACHING OF THE WORD

The following exercise is designed to help you examine the way you hear and respond to the Word of God when it is proclaimed. Put a check next to each question where the Holy Spirit convicts you of an area of need in your life. Ask God to make you a hearer and a doer of His Word.

How Well Do I Listen to the Word?

ANOINTED EARS ARE AS ESSENTIAL AS ANOINTED TONGUES. WE SHOULD CRY FOR THE BAPTISM OF THE SPIRIT FOR HEARING AS WELL AS FOR THE BAPTISM OF THE SPIRIT FOR SPEAKING.[1]
—E. M. BOUNDS

15

"Speak, for your servant is listening." —1 Samuel 3:10

- ☐ Do I delight to hear the Word proclaimed? (Psalm 119:16)

- ☐ Do I expect God to speak to me every time I hear His Word proclaimed? (Jer. 29:13)

- ☐ Do I tremble at the Word of the Lord? (Isa. 66:2; Ezra 9:4)

- ☐ Do I pray for those who proclaim the Word to me, that they might be pure, anointed vessels of God? (1 Thess. 5:25)

How Well Do I Respond to the Word?

A GOOD HEARER IS A DOER OF THE WORD. HIS WEEKDAY LIFE IS AN APPLICATION AND REPRODUCTION OF THE LAST SABBATH SERMON, AND THIS GIVES HIM GOOD READINESS FOR THE NEXT HEARING.[2] —E.M. BOUNDS

For we also have received the good news just as they did. But the message they heard did not benefit them, since they were not united with those who heard it in faith. —Hebrews 4:2

- ☐ Do I respond in faith, that is, acting on the Word I have heard? (Heb. 4:2)

- ☐ Am I willing to let the message sit in judgment

of me rather than my sitting in judgment of the message? (Psalm 139:23–24)

☐ Do I take the message personally rather than thinking of how it applies to those around me? (James 1:21)

☐ Do I pass on to others what I have learned from the Word of God? (1 Thess. 1:8)

☐ Am I quick to respond in humility and obedience when the light of His Word exposes spiritual need or darkness in my life? (2 Kings 22:11, 19)

FOR THOSE WHO TEACH OR PREACH THE WORD

The biblical standards for those who preach the Word can be applied not only to those who pastor churches and stand behind pulpits but also to those who teach Sunday school classes, lead Bible studies, and minister the Word in a variety of settings.

The following exercise is designed to help those of us who proclaim the Word examine our ministries in the light of God's standard. Put a check next to each question where the Holy Spirit convicts you of an area of need in your life or ministry. Then take time to prayerfully read the related Scriptures and to ask God to make you a more faithful and fruitful servant.

Personal Life Message

THE MESSAGE MUST BE PART OF OURSELVES.... OUR LIVES MUST BE THE SACRAMENT OF THE MESSAGE.... BEFORE GOD'S MESSAGE CAN LIBERATE OTHER SOULS, THE LIBERATION MUST BE REAL IN YOU.[3] —OSWALD CHAMBERS

You are witnesses, and so is God, of how devoutly, righteously, and blamelessly we conducted ourselves with you believers.
—1 Thessalonians 2:10

☐ Does my life back up and illustrate the truths that I teach? (1 Thess. 1:5)

☐ Do I seek to personally apply the Word to my own life before proclaiming it to others? (James 3:1)

☐ Is the Word consistently transforming my life? (1 Tim. 4:16)

Preparation

WHEN YOU YOURSELF ARE GRIPPED AND MOVED IN THE PREPARATION YOU WILL GENERALLY FIND THAT THE SAME HAPPENS IN THE PREACHING. IT IS WHEN YOU HAVE BEEN STIRRED IN THIS WAY, WHEN THE MESSAGE YOU ARE PREPARING COMES WITH POWER TO YOU, AND DOES SOMETHING TO YOU, THAT IT IS LIKELY TO DO THE SAME TO THE PEOPLE.[4]
—D. MARTYN LLOYD-JONES

19

Now Ezra had determined in his heart to study the law of the LORD, obey it, and teach its statutes and ordinances in Israel.
—Ezra 7:10

☐ Do I spend adequate time in study and preparation? (2 Tim. 2:15)

☐ Do I spend time in prayer, asking God to open my eyes and heart, and asking Him to open the eyes and hearts of those who hear? (Eph. 1:16–18)

☐ Do I pray for those to whom I am ministering? (Phil. 1:9–11)

☐ Do I wait on the Lord to know what He would have me teach? (John 12:49)

☐ Do I first listen to what God wants to say to me before attempting to speak on His behalf to others? (Ezek. 3:1; 1 Sam 3:21–4:1)

Proclamation

YOU CAN HAVE KNOWLEDGE, AND YOU CAN BE METICULOUS IN YOUR PREPARATION. BUT WITHOUT THE UNCTION OF THE HOLY SPIRIT YOU WILL HAVE NO POWER, AND YOUR PREACHING WILL NOT BE EFFECTIVE.[5] —D. MARTYN LLOYD-JONES

My speech and my preaching were not with persuasive words of wisdom but with a demonstration of the Spirit's power.
—1 Corinthians 2:4

☐ Do I communicate God's truth with conviction, fervency, and passion? Do I preach earnestly, in a way that people can tell I believe what I am saying? (2 Cor. 5:20)

☐ Is my communication characterized by sobriety rather than looseness or frivolity in a way that is appropriate for dealing with eternal issues? (Titus 2:1)

☐ Do I actually read the Word of God to the people rather than merely communicating my own words about His Word? (Josh. 8:34–35; 1 Tim. 4:13)

☐ Do I communicate the truth clearly, helping people to understand the meaning of the Word? (Neh. 8:8)

☐ Do I pray for and seek the anointing of the Holy Spirit on my public ministry? (Luke 4:18; Acts 1:8)

☐ Am I providing a balanced diet for my people by proclaiming the whole counsel of God, not just the portions of Scripture that are easy to swallow? (Acts 20:27)

☐ In proclaiming the Word, do I use methods that enhance the message rather than merely entertaining my audience? (2 Tim. 2:16; 4:3)

☐ Am I more concerned about ministering in the power of the Holy Spirit than about impressing my hearers with my eloquence or communication skills? (1 Cor. 2:4)

☐ Do I make personal, direct, and practical application of the Word to people's lives? (1 Thess. 5:14–18)

☐ Do I earnestly appeal to people to respond to the truth? (2 Cor. 5:20)

☐ Am I faithful to warn my hearers of the dangers of neglecting the truth? (Heb. 2:1–3)

☐ Am I willing to speak the truth even when I know it may "ruffle feathers"? (Ezek. 2:6–7)

☐ Am I willing, when necessary, to directly and specifically confront sin in the Body rather than brushing it under the carpet? (1 Cor. 4:21–5:13)

Heart Attitudes and Motives

TO LOVE TO PREACH IS ONE THING; TO LOVE THOSE TO WHOM WE PREACH QUITE ANOTHER.[6] —RICHARD CECIL

22

For our exhortation didn't come from error or impurity or an intent to deceive. Instead, just as we have been approved by God to be entrusted with the gospel, so we speak, not to please people, but rather God, who examines our hearts. For we never used flattering speech, as you know, or had greedy motives—God is our witness—and we didn't seek glory from people, either from you or from others. —1 Thessalonians 2:3–6

☐ Do I consider it a privilege to have been set apart by God for the ministry of the gospel? Do I express gratitude for that calling? (1 Tim. 1:12)

☐ Are my motives pure? Do I long for God's approval more than the approval of men? Am I more concerned about pleasing God than impressing my audience? (1 Thess. 2:4, 6; Gal. 1:10)

☐ Do I genuinely love and care for the people to whom I am ministering? (1 Thess. 2:8)

☐ Do I receive criticism with a spirit of humility? (Phil. 2:5)

☐ Am I willing to endure rejection, if necessary, for proclaiming the truth? (1 Cor. 4:9, 13; 1 Thess. 2:2)

☐ Do I reflect any human commendation or praise back to God? (2 Cor. 3:4–5)

☐ Do I ever weep over the lives and needs of my "flock"? (Acts 20:31; 2 Cor. 2:4)

☐ Do I grieve over those who are still unrepentant and separated from Christ? (Rom. 9:2–3)

☐ Am I dependent upon the power of the Holy Spirit to illuminate the Word to His people, to quicken their hearts with conviction, and to enable them to obey? (1 Cor. 2:10–16)

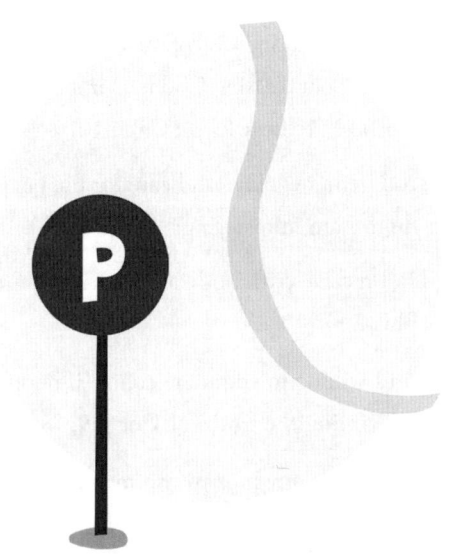

FOLLOW THE LEADER
How to Bless Your Spiritual Leaders

God's Word identifies the requirements for those in positions of spiritual leadership. It also speaks to the attitudes and actions we are to display toward our spiritual leaders. Use the following passages and questions to help evaluate how well you are fulfilling your responsibilities as a follower.

Now we ask you, brothers and sisters, to give recognition to those who labor among you and lead you in the Lord and admonish you, and to regard them very highly in love because of their work. Be at peace among yourselves. —1 Thessalonians 5:12–13

- Do I regularly take time to recognize my spiritual leaders and to identify the contributions they have made in my life?

25

- Do I respect those who minister spiritually to me?
- Do I express appreciation and gratitude to my spiritual leaders for their labor on my behalf?
- Do I speak well of my spiritual leaders to others?

The elders who are good leaders are to be considered worthy of double honor, especially those who work hard at preaching and teaching. For the Scripture says: Do not muzzle an ox while it is treading out the grain, and, "The worker is worthy of his wages." —1 Timothy 5:17–18

- Do I express honor in tangible, practical ways to those who lead me spiritually and minister the Word of God to me and to my family?
- Are the financial needs of the pastoral staff in our church being adequately met?
- Have I invested in the lives of those who have discipled and helped me grow in my walk with God?

Let the one who is taught the word share all his good things with the teacher. —Galatians 6:6

- Am I investing into the lives of those who teach me the Word?
- Do I look for opportunities to minister to the practical needs of my spiritual leaders?

26

- Do I reach out to encourage the leaders in my church when something they've done or taught is a blessing to me?

Remember your leaders who have spoken God's word to you. As you carefully observe the outcome of their lives, imitate their faith. —Hebrews 13:7

- Do I seek to learn from the lives of my spiritual leaders?
- Do I pay attention to godly characteristics in the lives of those who have taught me the Word of God? What examples have they set that I can follow?
- Do I pray for my pastors to continue to grow in Christlike character?

Obey your leaders and submit to them, since they keep watch over your souls as those who will give an account, so that they can do this with joy and not with grief, for that would be unprofitable for you. —Hebrews 13:17

- Am I spiritually accountable to anyone in a position of spiritual authority? Do I allow anyone to "watch for my soul"?
- Am I responsive to the direction of my spiritual leaders?
- When my spiritual leaders stand before God to give account for my life, will they be able to do so with joy?

For whenever someone says, "I belong to Paul," and another, "I belong to Apollos," are you not acting like mere humans? What then is Apollos? What is Paul? They are servants through whom you believed, and each has the role the Lord has given. I planted, Apollos watered, but God gave the growth.

—1 Corinthians 3:4–6

- Am I careful to give God the glory for the spiritual growth and fruit in my life?
- Am I careful to avoid exalting one spiritual leader above others?
- Do I realize that ultimately it is God who is at work in my life and that those men who have most impacted me are merely His servants?

First of all, then, I urge that petitions, prayers, intercessions, and thanksgivings be made for everyone, for kings and all those who are in authority, so that we may lead a tranquil and quiet life in all godliness and dignity. —1 Timothy 2:1–2

- Do I thank God for the leaders He has put in my life?
- Do I pray faithfully for the men who are in positions of spiritual leadership over my life?
- Do I take initiative to find out how I can pray for my spiritual leaders?

"PRAY FOR US!"

*Brothers and sisters, pray for us that the word of the Lord
may spread rapidly and be honored, just as it was with you.*
—2 Thessalonians 3:1

A Plea to Pray for Pastors
by Pastor Gardiner Spring

Let the thought sink deep into the heart of every church,
that their minister will be such a minister as their prayers
make him.

For who and what are the ministers themselves? Frail men,
fallible, sinning men, exposed to every snare, to temptation
in every form. And, from the post they occupy, they are
an easier target for the fiery darts of the foe. They are not
trite victims the great Adversary is seeking, when he would
wound and cripple Christ's ministers.

29

How perilous is the condition of that minister then, whose heart is not encouraged, whose hands are not strengthened, and who is not upheld by the prayers of his people!

It is at a fearful expense that ministers are ever allowed to enter the pulpit without being preceded, accompanied, and followed by the earnest prayers of the churches. It is no marvel that the pulpit is so powerless, and ministers so often disheartened when there are so few to hold up their hands.

When the churches cease to pray for ministers, ministers will no longer be a blessing to the churches.

"Brethren, pray for us!" Amen!

Gardiner Spring surrendered his life to ministry in the early 1800s. He went on to pastor Brick Presbyterian Church in New York City for sixty-three years. History records that the people of his church experienced "waves of revival" under his careful and consistent teaching of God's Word.

Among his many published writings and sermons, A Plea to Pray for Pastors *stands the test of time and continues to call us to lift our spiritual leaders up to the Lord in prayer.*[7]

A 30-DAY "PRAY FOR YOUR PASTOR" CHALLENGE

There is no greater gift you can give your pastor(s) and the spiritual leaders of your church than to pray for them.

Our pastors cannot win the battle alone; they need us to lift them up in fervent, specific prayer. After all, pastors are human—they face the same challenges that their people do, with some additional ones! They grow tired in ministry, are tempted to sin, and may find it difficult to balance their many roles and responsibilities. They need the encouragement and support of those they lead.

Imagine how the power of God might be released in our churches if we were to pray faithfully for our pastors.

If you want to encourage your spiritual leaders (and their wives!), let them know you are praying for them. Ask them periodically for any specific prayer requests and assure them you will pray accordingly.

Why not set aside one month every year for concentrated prayer for your pastor(s), other leaders in your church, and their families? Use the following prayer prompts as a guide.

Day 1

Pray that your pastor will love God with all his heart, soul, mind, and strength and that God's Spirit will continuously work in his heart. (Deut. 6:5; Matt. 6:33)

Day 2

Pray that your pastor will cultivate strong character and uncompromising integrity. Pray that his testimony will be genuine and that he will never do anything that he would need to hide from others. (1 Tim. 1:5; 3:7; Eph. 6:10–12)

Day 3

Pray for his personal walk with God—that his soul and spirit will be nourished and strengthened in his quiet time with God, beyond his sermon preparation. Pray that he will spend more time in the Word of God than reading Christian books and articles. (Mark 1:35; 2 Tim. 2:15–16)

Day 4

Pray that your pastor will counsel and teach with discernment through the wise use of Scripture and faith in God's power to work. Pray that he will be protected from the effects of sinful or negative attitudes that he encounters as he counsels. (James 1:5–6; John 17:15)

Day 5

Ask God to protect your pastor's marriage and keep it strong as a model of Christ's relationship with the Church. Pray that your pastor will tenderly cherish and lead his wife and that she will respect and encourage her husband, submitting to his leadership (Eph. 5:23–33). If your pastor is not married, pray for his relationships with loved ones and those who are close to them.

Day 6

Pray that God will protect your pastor's wife from bitterness when her husband is criticized. Pray that her prayer and devotional life will be consistent and that she will guard her mind and heart. (Heb. 12:15; Prov. 4:23)

Day 7

Pray for your pastor's children and especially that the pressures of the ministry will not discourage or embitter them.

Pray that your pastor will provide godly leadership in the home, not based on fear of what others will think but according to scriptural truth (Eph. 6:4; Col. 3:20–21). If your pastor does not have children, pray that God will give him many "spiritual children" as he shares the gospel.

Day 8

Ask God to protect your pastor from the evil plots of Satan. Pray that he will not be corrupted as he rubs shoulders with the world in the course of ministry. (John 17:15; Isa. 54:17; 2 Cor. 2:11; 1 Pet. 3:12; Psalm 9:9–10; 91:9–11)

Day 9

Pray that God will build a hedge of protection around your pastor's marriage and that he and his wife will be aware of the potential for any improper relationships. Pray that their family time will be protected. (2 Cor. 10:4–5; Matt. 19:6)

Day 10

Pray that your pastor will use discernment in his use of emails, the Internet, and social media. Ask God to guard his heart concerning the use of free time. Pray that he will be morally pure and that he will wear the armor of God so that he will not fall into sexual temptation. (Rom. 13:14; 1 Pet. 1:16; Eph. 6:10–18; 2 Cor. 10:4)

Day 11

Pray that God will bring wise friends and encouragers to your pastor and his family, to strengthen them for the ministry and provide meaningful fellowship and times of rest. (Phil. 2:19–25)

Day 12

Pray that your pastor will be humble and authentic in his faith, not given to pride or hypocrisy. Pray that he will have pure motives and give God glory for every gain or victory. (Mic. 6:8; Gal. 6:14; John 7:17–18; 1 Cor. 10:13)

Day 13

Pray that your pastor will make wise lifestyle choices in order to protect his health, especially in the areas of exercise, eating moderately, and getting sufficient rest. Pray for times of relaxation and renewal to balance the stress of ministry. (Rom. 12:1–2; 1 Cor. 6:19–20; 9:27; 10:13; James 3:1–2)

Day 14

Pray that your pastor will focus on the Word of God and walk in the fear of the Lord—rather than fear of man—as he prepares his messages. Pray that he will seek to please God rather than men and pursue holiness rather than the praise of men. (Acts 6:4; Prov. 19:23; 2 Tim. 2:15; Heb. 11:6; 2 Tim. 4:1–2)

Day 15

Praise God for your pastor's leadership and pray that he will make godly decisions. Pray that he will lead with a shepherd's heart and that he will always speak the truth in love. (1 Kings 3:9; 1 Pet. 5:2; Rom. 12:6–8; Jer. 3:15)

Day 16

Pray that your pastor will be courageous in the pulpit in proclaiming Christ and confident in his use of the Word of God. Ask God to help him preach with insight, transparency, and humility. (Col. 1:28; 4:3; Eph. 6:19)

Day 17

Pray that your pastor will be a "Great Commission man"—committed to personal evangelism and the equipping of the saints to seek the lost. Pray that he will have a heart to develop a thriving missions program in his church. (Rom. 10:15; Matt. 28:19–20; Luke 19:10)

Day 18

Pray that your pastor will be a man of prayer and worship and that he will lead by example—teaching the congregation how to walk in a close relationship with the Father. (1 Thess. 5:17; Acts 1:14; Matt. 4:10; Mark 1:35; Luke 22:46)

Day 19

Pray that your pastor will use wise time management and that he will seek God's perspective for his schedule, guarding his time against unnecessary interruptions. (Eph. 5:15–16; Col. 4:5; Psalm 90:12; John 9:4)

Day 20

Pray for a fresh divine anointing on your pastor's ministry. Pray that God's working will be powerfully evident both in his personal life and the spiritual life of the congregation. (1 Cor. 9:27; 2 Tim. 1:7; Rom. 15:18–19)

Day 21

Pray that your pastor will not give in to discouragement but will deal with inevitable criticism and conflict by committing himself into the hands of God, who judges righteously. (1 Pet. 2:23)

Day 22

Pray that your pastor will practice servant leadership, edifying the congregation with wisdom and serving with God's *agape* love. (Gal. 5:13; Eph. 6:7; Mark 10:43–45; Luke 9:23–24; John 13:5–9; Phil. 2:3–4)

Day 23

Pray for spiritual unity in the church staff and among the spiritual leadership of the church (elders, deacons, women's ministry leaders, etc.). Pray that the enemy will not be allowed to create division, strife, or misunderstanding among the church leaders. (1 John 4:11; Rom. 14:19; Eph. 4:1–16)

Day 24

Pray that God will give your pastor a clear, biblical vision of what your church can be and should be for His glory and that he will communicate that vision clearly and confidently to the church. (Prov. 29:18; John 15:16; 17:17; 2 Tim. 3:5)

Day 25

Pray that your pastor will seek God for personal revival and revival in your church and community. (2 Chron. 7:14; Psalm 69:32)

Day 26

Pray that your pastor will think biblically, with the mind of Christ. (1 Cor. 2:16; Col. 2:6–8; Eph. 4:17, 23–24)

Day 27

Pray that your pastor will earnestly seek God's will and be committed to instant and complete obedience—ready for God to work powerfully in and through his ministry. (2 Cor. 10:3–5; Luke 9:23–24)

Day 28

Pray that your pastor will be a man of faith and passionate love for God, not giving in to worries, fears, or an uptight and anxious spirit. (1 John 4:18; Prov. 3:5–6)

Day 29

Ask God to provide for the financial needs of your pastor and his family. Pray that he will be a wise steward of both personal finances and church funds. (Phil. 4:19; Heb. 13:5; 1 Tim. 6:11; Psalm 37:25)

Day 30

Ask God to heal any hurts that your pastor has suffered in the ministry. Pray that he will serve the Lord with gladness and encourage the congregation to worship God with a joyful, surrendered spirit. (Isa. 61:3)

NOTES

[1] E.M. Bounds, *Powerful and Prayerful Pulpits: Forty Days of Readings* (Grand Rapids, MI: Baker, 1993).

[2] Bounds, 226.

[3] Oswald Chambers, *My Utmost for His Highest* (Dodd, Mead & Company, 1935), March 10.

[4] D. Martyn Lloyd-Jones, *Preaching & Preachers* (Grand Rapids, MI: Zondervan, 1971), 299.

[5] Lloyd-Jones, 319.

[6] Richard Cecil, quoted in D. Martyn Lloyd-Jones, *Preaching & Preachers* (Grand Rapids, MI: Zondervan, 1971), 92.

[7] "Gardiner Spring," Banner of Truth (website), accessed August 17, 2022, www.banneroftruth.org/uk/about/banner-authors/gardiner-spring.